Mastering Spelling

Teacher's Resource Manual

discover friendship
freedom strangest
knowledge beginning
gathering character
thought power
peace discover vacation
borrowing

Level

A

GLOBE FEARON

Contents

REVIEWERS: Phyllis Aliberto, Port Chester-Rye Union Free School District, Port Chester, New York; **Karen L. Bennett,** Madera High School, Madera, California; **Cassandra E. Meltin,** M.A.T., J.D., Coordinator, Region 3 Chicago Public Schools, Chicago, Illinois; **Sally Parker,** M.A., Elk Grove Unified School District, Elk Grove, California; **ESL contributor: Jacqueline M. Córdova, Ph.D.,** California State University, Fullerton, California

Project Editor: Eleanor Ripp; **Production Editor:** Regina McAloney; **Interior Design:** Chris Callaway; **Cover Design:** Chris Callaway; **Electronic Page Production:** Mimi Raihl, Leslie Greenberg; **Editors:** Ayanna Taylor, Gina Dalessio

Printed in the United States of America
2 3 4 5 6 7 8 9 10 03 02 01 00 99

ISBN: 0-835-94875-7

GLOBE FEARON EDUCATIONAL PUBLISHER
Upper Saddle River, New Jersey
www.globefearon.com

Skills	Mastering Spelling Level	Be A Better Reader	World of Vocabulary	Success in Writing: Grammar
Phonics				
Recognizing syllables	A, B, C, D, F	A	Tan	
Dividing words into syllables	A, B, C, D, F	A, B, D, E, F		
Recognizing long and short vowel sounds	A, B, C, D	A	Tan	
Recognizing consonant blends	A, B, C, D	A	Tan	
Recognizing r-controlled vowel sounds	B	A		
Recognizing the accented syllable	A, B	A, B, C, D, E, F		
Recognizing the schwa sound	A, B, C			
Recognizing silent letters	A, B, E, F	B	Tan	
Recognizing vowel-consonant combinations	B, C, D, E, F	C		
Word Structure				
Recognizing prefixes, suffixes, and root words	A, B, C, D, E, F	A, E, F, G	Tan, Purple, Green	
Compound words	A, B, C, D, E, F			
Word Meanings				
Recognizing multiple meanings of words		A, C, E, F, G		
Adding prefixes to words	A, B, C, D, E, F	A, B, C, D, E, F	Tan	
Adding suffixes to words	A, B, C, D, E, F	A, B, C, D, E, F	Tan	
Understanding analogies	A, B, C, D	E, F, G	Aqua, Orange, Blue, Red, Purple, Green	
Understanding synonyms and antonyms	A, B, C, D	F	Yellow, Tan, Aqua, Orange, Blue, Red, Purple, Green	
Homophones	A, B, C, D, E		Yellow, Tan	Chapter 9

Skills	Mastering Spelling Level	Be A Better Reader	World of Vocabulary	Success in Writing: Grammar
Using the Dictionary				
Classifying	A, B, C, D	A, B, C, D, F		
Using alphabetical order	A, B, C, D, E, F	A, B	Yellow, Tan, Aqua, Orange, Blue, Red, Purple, Green	
Using guide words	B, D, E, F	A, B		
Using a dictionary entry	A, B, C, D, E, F	A, B, D, E, F		
Parts of Speech				
Nouns	A, B, C, D, E, F		Yellow, Tan, Orange, Blue, Purple, Green	Chapter 4
Singular and plural nouns	A, B, C, D, E, F			
Proper nouns	C, E, F			
Verbs	A, B, C, D, E, F		Yellow, Purple, Green	Chapter 4
Verb tense	A, B, C, D, E, F			Chapter 5
Irregular verbs	A			Chapter 5
Verb agreement	E			Chapter 5
Direct and indirect object	C, D			Chapter 5
Pronouns	A, C, D			Chapter 4
Adjectives	A, B, C, D, E, F		Yellow, Tan, Blue, Red, Purple, Green	Chapter 4
Adverbs	B, C, D, E, F		Purple, Green	Chapter 4
Prepositions	D			Chapter 4
Conjunctions	B, C, E			Chapter 4
Interjections	C			Chapter 4
Mechanics				
Capitalization	C, D, E, F		Yellow, Tan	Chapter 6
Abbreviations	B, E			
Apostrophes/ possessives	A, B, C, D, E, F		Blue, Red, Purple, Green	Chapter 6
Hyphens	C, E, F			Chapter 6
Spelling	A, B, C, D, E, F		Tan	Chapter 9
Spelling plurals	A, B, C, D, E, F		Yellow	Chapter 9
Contractions	A, B, D		Yellow, Tan	
Quotations	C			

Program Description

The Spelling Lesson

Part One: Introduction

The **Spelling Rule**, which states the spelling generalization targeted in the lesson, is introduced.

Students are then asked to **Say the Words**. In this section of the lesson, students are guided to listen for the target sound.

Students then **Write the Words** in categories. These categories are based on different sorting criteria designed to reinforce the spelling generalization targeted in the lesson. Students can compare their word sorts with partners, and should be encouraged to summarize in their own words the spelling generalization underlying their word sorts.

Students are encouraged to add several self-selected words to the list of study words. These may be words you suggest, words students frequently misspell in their own writing, or simply new words they discover that fit the lesson generalization. Students are always given some ideas as to where they might find additional words.

It is strongly recommended that you review the meanings of the study words so students are familiar with the vocabulary.

Part Two: Spelling and Language

The second major section of the lesson focuses on **Spelling and Language**. On this page, students complete two or three activities designed to help them relate their spelling words to grammar, usage, or the mechanics of writing.

These activities include:

- the formation of plurals and possessives
- the addition of prefixes or suffixes
- the formation of adjectives from nouns
- the formation of verbs from nouns
- changing the tense of a verb
- the formation of comparative adjectives
- writing rhyming words
- writing words from their phonetic spellings
- the formation of contractions
- writing irregular verbs

Mastering Spelling is a comprehensive spelling program designed to help students learn and apply spelling strategies. The program consists of Student Editions for six levels, Levels A–F, each accompanied by a Teacher Resource Manual. A comprehensive program Diagnosis and Placement Guide is available to help you determine students' appropriate level of placement. Within each level are 26 lessons with 15 words presented in each.

Lessons are based on spelling concepts that are derived from one of the following:

(1) phonics generalizations

(2) structural analysis (prefixes, suffixes, roots, formation of plurals), or

(3) word study (homophones, contractions, compound words, related words, and words from other languages)

Within each level, the spelling lists have been carefully compiled from research-generated word lists that rank words by their frequency of occurrence in reading and writing, and how often they are misspelled.

Each of the 26 lessons in the Student Edition contains four parts and is designed to be used with teacher guidance or independently.

The ***Did You Know?*** feature in this section of the lesson focuses students' attention on fascinating facts about the history of a study word. In this feature, students explore the derivation of words and the ways in which our language continues to evolve and change over time.

Part Three: Build Vocabulary

This section helps students focus on the meaning or meanings of each study word presented in the lesson. Activities include:

- writing study words that match clues or definitions
- writing study words in meaning categories with related words
- completing analogies
- completing sentences
- writing synonyms and antonyms

The ***Real-Life Spelling*** feature presents a number of study words in a real-life context, such as a to-do list, a journal entry, an advertisement, a video review, an e-mail message, a travel brochure, a Yellow Pages ad, or a book jacket. Students use their study words to complete sentences, correct misspelled words, or answer questions about the writing sample.

Part Four: Spelling Review

In the final section of the lesson, a ***Spelling Review*** provides a structured review opportunity for students to write all their study words once more. Students complete crossword puzzles, charts, word search puzzles, acrostics, word pyramids, scrambled letter puzzles, secret codes, and clueless crossword puzzles.

The ***Spelling and Writing*** section of the lesson provides students with a writing prompt and a prewriting suggestion to help them focus and organize their ideas. The writing assignment relates directly to the writing sample previously presented in the ***Real-Life Spelling*** feature, which is a model for students' own writing.

Using Mastering Spelling

Begin each lesson with a spelling pretest. Research indicates that students benefit most from self-correcting their own pretests and noting any trouble spots in the words they miss. Administer the pretest by stating a word, using the word in a sentence, and restating the word. Following the pretest, students can move into their Student Edition and proceed through the four-page lesson. Students can use their spelling books every day or periodically throughout a week to complete the four pages of the lesson, with time for writing on their own.

In most classrooms, students will conclude the lesson by taking a final test of the 15 study words and any additional words they have targeted for individual study. Some teachers give a dictated spelling test each week. Note that for every two lessons, reproducible tests are provided in this Teacher's Resource Manual. These tests employ a variety of formats like those students will encounter on standardized tests.

The Spelling Dictionary

At the back of each level is a comprehensive spelling dictionary that includes a Pronunciation Key, a sample entry, and entries for all of the study words in the level. Following each entry word is its phonetic respelling, the word's part of speech, and one or more definitions of the word. The page number at the end of each entry refers students back to the lesson in which the word was introduced. You may wish to guide students through the diagram on page 106 showing how to use a dictionary entry, and through the brief explanation of the dictionary's pronunciation key on page 107.

Other self-help pages found at the back of the Student Edition include a brief description of the writing process on page 125, and tips for how to successfully prepare for and take a writing test on page 126. On the inside back cover, students will find a handy reminder of study steps for effectively studying a spelling word, as well as a summary of other useful strategies for remembering how to spell a word.

Second Language Learners and English Spelling

Spelling in English poses significant challenges for large numbers of native speakers of English. These problems escalate enormously for second language learners. Teachers of non-native speakers of English should be alert to students' problems, which include—but are not limited to—the following:

- Second language learners are acquiring new vocabulary and sentence structures. As students work with a spelling program, teachers can point out word meanings and contextual usages as well as basic elements of spelling.

- Phonemes differ from one language to another. Second language learners may have difficulties with phonetic generalizations, since they hear and pronounce a different set of phonemes. It is first necessary to provide listening practice to help the students distinguish the sounds of English, and then to make the link to the written forms by attending to the visual elements of words. In addition, second language learners need extra guidance with dictionary respelling keys.

- Sound-symbol correspondences frequently differ across languages that use the same writing system. For example, in Spanish the letter *h* is an historical vestige but now represents no sound unless found in the *ch* combination. Written Hawaiian uses the letter *w* to represent the sound of *v*. Teachers should be aware that students frequently use the spelling conventions of their own language(s) when writing English. They should use this awareness to guide students to use those sound-symbol correspondences that are appropriate for English.

- Mideastern languages such as Hebrew and Arabic use different writing systems with their own unique diacritical marks to indicate vowels. Students from such language backgrounds may need more guided practice with English vowel, diphthong, and tripthong spellings. Encouraging them to add new words of their own that belong to each spelling group is a helpful technique.

- Some students speak and write languages that employ ideographs (i.e., Japanese, Chinese). In such languages, sound-symbol correspondences do not occur; instead, each character represents an idea. Sometimes these students will use the strategy of learning groups of sight words rather than doing phonetic analysis. Teachers may suggest that these students make lists of rhyming words having similar spelling patterns (i.e., **name**, **game**, **tame**, **lame**) and then guide students to find the common elements and apply them when appropriate.

- Learning styles vary across cultures. Students from many other countries are trained to memorize and learn by rote. They may excel in spelling tests in which the study words are dictated in the order learned; however, they will falter when confronted with different formats. Second language students need extra help in recognizing words in different environments and should be encouraged to make individual flash cards to help them study.

Spelling Rules and Generalizations

Second language learners need explicit instruction to help them with rule-based spelling. For generations, English speakers have recited such rules as "*i* before *e* except after *c*" and "Change *-y* to *-i* and add *-es.*" These rules work for native speakers of English because they already have a substantial vocabulary and can be led rather quickly to see similarities between examples that are already in their vocabulary bank. For the second language learner, however, each new word is an individual entity at first; only as the student grows more proficient in English can the rules be successfully exploited. Pairing English language learners with students who are more proficient English speakers to complete written exercise is a useful strategy.

Teachers who help students hear the new language first and who provide guided practice, use pairs and peer tutoring, and offer visual clues will be gratified by the positive results.

Read each group of words. Mark the circle next to the word that is spelled correctly.

1. Ⓐ chace
   Ⓑ chas
   Ⓒ chase
   Ⓓ chais

2. Ⓐ silence
   Ⓑ silance
   Ⓒ sighlence
   Ⓓ sylence

3. Ⓐ plese
   Ⓑ please
   Ⓒ pleese
   Ⓓ pleaze

4. Ⓐ oder
   Ⓑ odur
   Ⓒ odir
   Ⓓ odor

5. Ⓐ statment
   Ⓑ statemint
   Ⓒ statement
   Ⓓ staitment

6. Ⓐ frite
   Ⓑ freigt
   Ⓒ frigt
   Ⓓ fright

7. Ⓐ treet
   Ⓑ treat
   Ⓒ trete
   Ⓓ treate

8. Ⓐ pirate
   Ⓑ pirat
   Ⓒ pyrate
   Ⓓ pirit

9. Ⓐ afrade
   Ⓑ affraid
   Ⓒ affrade
   Ⓓ afraid

10. Ⓐ heighest
    Ⓑ highest
    Ⓒ hyest
    Ⓓ hiest

11. Ⓐ wheils
    Ⓑ whiels
    Ⓒ wheels
    Ⓓ weehls

12. Ⓐ bacon
    Ⓑ baycon
    Ⓒ baicon
    Ⓓ bacun

13. Ⓐ spyder
    Ⓑ spidur
    Ⓒ spider
    Ⓓ spidar

14. Ⓐ evan
    Ⓑ even
    Ⓒ evin
    Ⓓ evun

15. Ⓐ hoetel
    Ⓑ hotel
    Ⓒ hootel
    Ⓓ hotell

16. Ⓐ these
    Ⓑ thees
    Ⓒ theaz
    Ⓓ theze

17. Ⓐ stanes
    Ⓑ steans
    Ⓒ stayns
    Ⓓ stains

18. Ⓐ lyfetime
    Ⓑ liftime
    Ⓒ lifetime
    Ⓓ lifetyme

19. Ⓐ compleat
    Ⓑ compleet
    Ⓒ complet
    Ⓓ complete

20. Ⓐ flavor
    Ⓑ flayvor
    Ⓒ flaivor
    Ⓓ flaver

21. Ⓐ elbow
    Ⓑ ellbow
    Ⓒ elbo
    Ⓓ elboe

22. Ⓐ spyne
    Ⓑ spine
    Ⓒ sppine
    Ⓓ speine

23. Ⓐ gready
    Ⓑ greede
    Ⓒ gredy
    Ⓓ greedy

24. Ⓐ iseberg
    Ⓑ icebirg
    Ⓒ iceberg
    Ⓓ iceburg

25. Ⓐ reecent
    Ⓑ recent
    Ⓒ reicent
    Ⓓ reacent

Name ____ **Spelling Test 2**

Read each sentence. Mark the circle to indicate the misspelled word. Mark circle D if there are no mistakes.

1. Ⓐ Ⓑ Ⓒ Ⓓ I used a <u>pencil</u> to draw a <u>spirel</u> in the <u>middle</u> of my paper.
                          A   B   C

2. Ⓐ Ⓑ Ⓒ Ⓓ Dad gave him a <u>nickel</u> to pick up the spilled <u>gravel</u> with a <u>shoval</u>.
                          A   B   C

3. Ⓐ Ⓑ Ⓒ Ⓓ <u>Apral</u> is a <u>wonderful</u> <u>month</u> to see spring flowers.
       A   B   C

4. Ⓐ Ⓑ Ⓒ Ⓓ Blow with a <u>steady</u> <u>breath</u> to make a big <u>bubble</u>.
                   A   B   C

5. Ⓐ Ⓑ Ⓒ Ⓓ You can <u>trust</u> her to be <u>loyal</u> and <u>plessant</u>.
               A   B   C

6. Ⓐ Ⓑ Ⓒ Ⓓ If you <u>spred</u> oil on a <u>leather</u> mitt, it will not crack or <u>crumble</u>.
                  A   B   C

7. Ⓐ Ⓑ Ⓒ Ⓓ Some sodas <u>sparkle</u> and <u>tickul</u> your <u>tongue</u>.
                    A   B   C

Read each group of phrases. Mark the circle next to the phrase with the word that is misspelled.

8. Ⓐ a steam <u>shovel</u>
  Ⓑ an <u>April</u> shower
  Ⓒ <u>spiral</u> lines
  Ⓓ <u>bunnch</u> of bananas

9. Ⓐ <u>touched</u> the book
  Ⓑ the <u>suthern</u> route
  Ⓒ <u>trust</u> your friend
  Ⓓ a pink <u>tongue</u>

10. Ⓐ the <u>uther</u> girl
  Ⓑ last <u>month</u>
  Ⓒ <u>wonderful</u> ideas
  Ⓓ a quick <u>breath</u>

11. Ⓐ <u>spread</u> its wings
  Ⓑ <u>pleasant</u> visits
  Ⓒ a long <u>frendship</u>
  Ⓓ an annoying <u>sniffle</u>

12. Ⓐ a team <u>huddle</u>
  Ⓑ two <u>helthy</u> snacks
  Ⓒ playful <u>tickle</u>
  Ⓓ the <u>other</u> group

13. Ⓐ the <u>lether</u> belt
  Ⓑ <u>touched</u> her toes
  Ⓒ <u>southern</u> accents
  Ⓓ <u>bunch</u> of grapes

14. Ⓐ <u>shovel</u> snow
  Ⓑ <u>pleasant</u> people
  Ⓒ hold her <u>tongue</u>
  Ⓓ <u>stedy</u> rain

15. Ⓐ <u>trust</u> to luck
  Ⓑ a <u>bunch</u> of flowers
  Ⓒ the furry <u>mammel</u>
  Ⓓ <u>wonderful</u> surprises

16. Ⓐ my <u>other</u> coat
  Ⓑ in a <u>month</u>
  Ⓒ our long <u>friendship</u>
  Ⓓ <u>loyel</u> partners

17. Ⓐ a sharp <u>pencel</u>
  Ⓑ a deep <u>breath</u>
  Ⓒ <u>healthy</u> pets
  Ⓓ <u>leather</u> purses

18. Ⓐ one shiny <u>nickle</u>
  Ⓑ <u>steady</u> dripping
  Ⓒ <u>touched</u> the floor
  Ⓓ the young <u>mammal</u>

19. Ⓐ <u>spiral</u> staircases
  Ⓑ loads of <u>gravil</u>
  Ⓒ a red <u>pencil</u>
  Ⓓ my last <u>nickel</u>

20. Ⓐ <u>southern</u> foods
  Ⓑ break and <u>crumble</u>
  Ⓒ a soap <u>bubbel</u>
  Ⓓ <u>gravel</u> pits

21. Ⓐ the shortest <u>friendship</u>
  Ⓑ <u>healthy</u> eating habits
  Ⓒ <u>spread</u> the frosting
  Ⓓ a bad <u>snifful</u>

22. Ⓐ <u>loyal</u> supporter
  Ⓑ a tight <u>huddal</u>
  Ⓒ one day in <u>April</u>
  Ⓓ the <u>middle</u> row

23. Ⓐ in another <u>month</u>
  Ⓑ <u>sparkle</u> brightly
  Ⓒ <u>crumbul</u> into pieces
  Ⓓ a soft <u>sniffle</u>

24. Ⓐ <u>tickle</u> her toes
  Ⓑ red <u>leather</u> shoes
  Ⓒ a colored <u>pencil</u>
  Ⓓ shine and <u>sparkal</u>

25. Ⓐ the one in the <u>middul</u>
  Ⓑ a flying <u>mammal</u>
  Ⓒ <u>huddle</u> in a corner
  Ⓓ <u>bursting</u> a bubble

Read each group of phrases. Mark the circle next to the phrase with the misspelled word.

1. Ⓐ spilling the milk
   Ⓑ orderring lunch
   Ⓒ borrowing her book
   Ⓓ gathering the apples

2. Ⓐ an itche rash
   Ⓑ a breezy evening
   Ⓒ cheating in a game
   Ⓓ wrinkly clothing

3. Ⓐ smoky candles
   Ⓑ spending her savings
   Ⓒ a stubby pencil
   Ⓓ sugesting an idea

4. Ⓐ a bony chicken
   Ⓑ sandy beaches
   Ⓒ one fogy day
   Ⓓ a shaky chair

5. Ⓐ caching a cold
   Ⓑ a starry night
   Ⓒ salty peanuts
   Ⓓ spilling her drink

6. Ⓐ ordering tickets
   Ⓑ a filthee mess
   Ⓒ wavy lines
   Ⓓ bothering her mother

7. Ⓐ a twisting line of dancers
   Ⓑ lacy snowflakes
   Ⓒ misty and foggy
   Ⓓ openning a package

8. Ⓐ cheating and lying
   Ⓑ spending money
   Ⓒ lacee cuffs
   Ⓓ the opening paragraph

9. Ⓐ gathering clouds
   Ⓑ filthy hands
   Ⓒ a speading ticket
   Ⓓ itchy mosquito bites

10. Ⓐ the stary skies
    Ⓑ twisting her hair
    Ⓒ shaky ground
    Ⓓ a smoky room

11. Ⓐ a bony fish
    Ⓑ catching a ball
    Ⓒ training camp
    Ⓓ a teeching job

12. Ⓐ a shakey table
    Ⓑ opening the door
    Ⓒ scaly snakes
    Ⓓ a lacy blouse

13. Ⓐ bothering the baby
    Ⓑ salty popcorn
    Ⓒ a speeding car
    Ⓓ spendding her free time

14. Ⓐ teaching the class
    Ⓑ wavey hair
    Ⓒ bony fingers
    Ⓓ suggesting an answer

15. Ⓐ directing traffic
    Ⓑ twisting in the wind
    Ⓒ catching a bug
    Ⓓ a breezey day

16. Ⓐ foggy glasses
    Ⓑ trainning wheels
    Ⓒ ordering from a menu
    Ⓓ a scaly lizard

17. Ⓐ salty meat
    Ⓑ itchy spot
    Ⓒ a stuby bottle
    Ⓓ opening a present

18. Ⓐ a filthy rag
    Ⓑ a sandey cove
    Ⓒ suggesting a book
    Ⓓ borrowing a towel

19. Ⓐ cheeting on a test
    Ⓑ a lacy collar
    Ⓒ training a dog
    Ⓓ a wavy design

20. Ⓐ a starry design
    Ⓑ spilling the water
    Ⓒ a saltee taste
    Ⓓ wrinkly skin

21. Ⓐ a breezy answer
    Ⓑ directing a movie
    Ⓒ a shaky voice
    Ⓓ twistting in the wind

22. Ⓐ teaching the children
    Ⓑ wrinkely cloth
    Ⓒ suggesting a color
    Ⓓ a smoky fire

23. Ⓐ gathering at the corner
    Ⓑ catching a fish
    Ⓒ directting a play
    Ⓓ a filthy room

24. Ⓐ scaley patches
    Ⓑ speeding traffic
    Ⓒ bothering the class
    Ⓓ a smoky taste

25. Ⓐ sandy footprints
    Ⓑ boney legs
    Ⓒ a stubby crayon
    Ⓓ borrowing a tape

Read each group of words. Mark the circle next to the misspelled word.

1. Ⓐ admitting
   Ⓑ he'll
   Ⓒ sh'ell
   Ⓓ beginning

2. Ⓐ slaping
   Ⓑ wasn't
   Ⓒ permitting
   Ⓓ won't

3. Ⓐ preferring
   Ⓑ arn't
   Ⓒ couldn't
   Ⓓ outrunning

4. Ⓐ can't
   Ⓑ bragging
   Ⓒ doesn't
   Ⓓ ocuring

5. Ⓐ upsetting
   Ⓑ don't
   Ⓒ forgetting
   Ⓓ hazn't

6. Ⓐ snipeing
   Ⓑ who'd
   Ⓒ splitting
   Ⓓ we've

7. Ⓐ gripping
   Ⓑ izn't
   Ⓒ weren't
   Ⓓ throbbing

8. Ⓐ they've
   Ⓑ couldn't
   Ⓒ ploting
   Ⓓ snipping

9. Ⓐ hasn't
   Ⓑ occurring
   Ⓒ aren't
   Ⓓ thay've

10. Ⓐ slapping
    Ⓑ throbing
    Ⓒ she'll
    Ⓓ plotting

11. Ⓐ wern't
    Ⓑ he'll
    Ⓒ preferring
    Ⓓ wasn't

12. Ⓐ doesn't
    Ⓑ gripeing
    Ⓒ she'll
    Ⓓ who'd

13. Ⓐ we'ave
    Ⓑ slapping
    Ⓒ occurring
    Ⓓ hasn't

14. Ⓐ spliting
    Ⓑ isn't
    Ⓒ aren't
    Ⓓ snipping

15. Ⓐ they've
    Ⓑ gripping
    Ⓒ who'ld
    Ⓓ throbbing

16. Ⓐ weren't
    Ⓑ plotting
    Ⓒ we've
    Ⓓ forgeting

17. Ⓐ do'nt
    Ⓑ bragging
    Ⓒ who'd
    Ⓓ splitting

18. Ⓐ gripping
    Ⓑ upseting
    Ⓒ outrunning
    Ⓓ doesn't

19. Ⓐ couldn't
    Ⓑ we've
    Ⓒ weren't
    Ⓓ braging

20. Ⓐ forgetting
    Ⓑ don't
    Ⓒ can'nt
    Ⓓ preferring

21. Ⓐ upsetting
    Ⓑ permitting
    Ⓒ coudn't
    Ⓓ wasn't

22. Ⓐ wo'nt
    Ⓑ beginning
    Ⓒ admitting
    Ⓓ he'll

23. Ⓐ isn't
    Ⓑ slapping
    Ⓒ hasn't
    Ⓓ permiting

24. Ⓐ occurring
    Ⓑ begining
    Ⓒ aren't
    Ⓓ she'll

25. Ⓐ can't
    Ⓑ outrunning
    Ⓒ admiting
    Ⓓ won't

Read each group of words. Mark the circle next to the word that is spelled correctly.

1. Ⓐ advize
   Ⓑ advice
   Ⓒ adviece
   Ⓓ advis

2. Ⓐ inshult
   Ⓑ insilt
   Ⓒ incult
   Ⓓ insult

3. Ⓐ chose
   Ⓑ choze
   Ⓒ chooze
   Ⓓ choce

4. Ⓐ purson
   Ⓑ persen
   Ⓒ person
   Ⓓ persun

5. Ⓐ bought
   Ⓑ bawt
   Ⓒ boght
   Ⓓ booght

6. Ⓐ sootcase
   Ⓑ suitcas
   Ⓒ suitcase
   Ⓓ suitkase

7. Ⓐ roat
   Ⓑ wroat
   Ⓒ wroote
   Ⓓ wrote

8. Ⓐ sciense
   Ⓑ science
   Ⓒ sciunce
   Ⓓ siance

9. Ⓐ desend
   Ⓑ descend
   Ⓒ discend
   Ⓓ disend

10. Ⓐ sleeped
    Ⓑ sleept
    Ⓒ slept
    Ⓓ slipt

11. Ⓐ muscle
    Ⓑ musal
    Ⓒ musel
    Ⓓ musil

12. Ⓐ tor
    Ⓑ toor
    Ⓒ toar
    Ⓓ tore

13. Ⓐ sissors
    Ⓑ sissers
    Ⓒ scissors
    Ⓓ scissurs

14. Ⓐ built
    Ⓑ bilt
    Ⓒ billt
    Ⓓ biult

15. Ⓐ harmles
    Ⓑ harmless
    Ⓒ harmliss
    Ⓓ hermless

16. Ⓐ tawt
    Ⓑ taugt
    Ⓒ tawght
    Ⓓ taught

17. Ⓐ grassy
    Ⓑ grasy
    Ⓒ grassey
    Ⓓ grasee

18. Ⓐ akross
    Ⓑ acros
    Ⓒ akross
    Ⓓ across

19. Ⓐ spok
    Ⓑ spoak
    Ⓒ spoke
    Ⓓ spowk

20. Ⓐ progres
    Ⓑ progress
    Ⓒ progess
    Ⓓ progris

21. Ⓐ cawt
    Ⓑ caut
    Ⓒ caught
    Ⓓ kaught

22. Ⓐ icikle
    Ⓑ icickle
    Ⓒ sicle
    Ⓓ icicle

23. Ⓐ crept
    Ⓑ krept
    Ⓒ creapt
    Ⓓ cript

24. Ⓐ cerial
    Ⓑ cereal
    Ⓒ sereal
    Ⓓ cereel

25. Ⓐ ansestor
    Ⓑ ancester
    Ⓒ ancestor
    Ⓓ anncestor

Read each sentence. Mark the circle to indicate the misspelled word. Mark circle D if there are no mistakes.

1. Ⓐ Ⓑ Ⓒ Ⓓ During the <u>hottest</u> weather, it's important to wear your <u>loosest</u> <u>cloze</u>.
               A   B   C

2. Ⓐ Ⓑ Ⓒ Ⓓ The <u>largest</u> <u>zebra</u> had <u>zigag</u> stripes.
            A   B   C

3. Ⓐ Ⓑ Ⓒ Ⓓ I <u>advize</u> you not to <u>refuse</u> to answer the <u>buzzer</u>.
        A   B   C

4. Ⓐ Ⓑ Ⓒ Ⓓ Her <u>present</u> is <u>supposed</u> to be in one of these <u>packages</u>.
        A   B   C

5. Ⓐ Ⓑ Ⓒ Ⓓ Mom will <u>freeze</u> the <u>larjer</u> of the leftover <u>dinners</u>.
            A   B   C

6. Ⓐ Ⓑ Ⓒ Ⓓ The musician played the <u>strangest</u> <u>jazz</u> tune on the <u>zylophone</u>.
                     A   B   C

7. Ⓐ Ⓑ Ⓒ Ⓓ The <u>wealthyest</u> man wore the <u>fanciest</u> <u>lizard</u> belt I had ever seen.
          A   B   C

Read each group of words. Mark the circle next to the word that is misspelled.

8. Ⓐ zigzag 　Ⓑ sillyer 　Ⓒ wealthier 　Ⓓ lizard	14. Ⓐ packages 　Ⓑ clothes 　Ⓒ dinners 　Ⓓ zebera	20. Ⓐ lose 　Ⓑ fancier 　Ⓒ advise 　Ⓓ precent
9. Ⓐ jazz 　Ⓑ fanciest 　Ⓒ buzzer 　Ⓓ wealthyer	15. Ⓐ fanciest 　Ⓑ hottest 　Ⓒ loosest 　Ⓓ buzer	21. Ⓐ madder 　Ⓑ strangest 　Ⓒ refuze 　Ⓓ freeze
10. Ⓐ supposed 　Ⓑ lose 　Ⓒ fanceyer 　Ⓓ clothes	16. Ⓐ madest 　Ⓑ refuse 　Ⓒ looser 　Ⓓ xylophone	22. Ⓐ larjest 　Ⓑ zigzag 　Ⓒ looser 　Ⓓ silliest
11. Ⓐ hoter 　Ⓑ madder 　Ⓒ present 　Ⓓ packages	17. Ⓐ larger 　Ⓑ jazs 　Ⓒ advise 　Ⓓ strangest	23. Ⓐ lizerd 　Ⓑ xylophone 　Ⓒ larger 　Ⓓ hotter
12. Ⓐ freeze 　Ⓑ silliest 　Ⓒ lous 　Ⓓ wealthiest	18. Ⓐ sillier 　Ⓑ lizard 　Ⓒ louser 　Ⓓ wealthiest	24. Ⓐ buzzer 　Ⓑ loosest 　Ⓒ dinners 　Ⓓ sillyer
13. Ⓐ jazz 　Ⓑ mader 　Ⓒ fancier 　Ⓓ hotter	19. Ⓐ zebra 　Ⓑ supposd 　Ⓒ sillier 　Ⓓ maddest	25. Ⓐ maddest 　Ⓑ hotest 　Ⓒ largest 　Ⓓ supposed

Name ____

Read each group of phrases. Mark the circle next to the phrase with the misspelled word.

1. Ⓐ large tree limb
   Ⓑ soda crackers
   Ⓒ dressed as a nome
   Ⓓ knowledge in a book

2. Ⓐ comb and brush
   Ⓑ sharp as a thumtack
   Ⓒ mark your calendar
   Ⓓ all twisted and gnarled

3. Ⓐ a kickball game
   Ⓑ climbed a mountain
   Ⓒ a dangerous chemical
   Ⓓ a klever answer

4. Ⓐ design a poster
   Ⓑ recipes in a cookbook
   Ⓒ an annoying gnat
   Ⓓ naw on a bone

5. Ⓐ red and black checkers
   Ⓑ read about a character
   Ⓒ kneel on the bench
   Ⓓ red hair and frekles

6. Ⓐ a bruised knuckle
   Ⓑ a loud eko
   Ⓒ clean the closet
   Ⓓ sit on a large tree limb

7. Ⓐ a pushpin or thumbtack
   Ⓑ a French cookbook
   Ⓒ sing in a korus
   Ⓓ knowledge about spiders

8. Ⓐ a computer keeboard
   Ⓑ turn the knob
   Ⓒ sweep the carpet
   Ⓓ covered with tiny freckles

9. Ⓐ a family custom
   Ⓑ go out on a limb
   Ⓒ a tiny nat
   Ⓓ a brave knight

10. Ⓐ num with cold
    Ⓑ played the part of a gnome
    Ⓒ check her calendar
    Ⓓ freckles on her nose

11. Ⓐ kneel before the king
    Ⓑ the narled tree
    Ⓒ coat closet
    Ⓓ teeth of a comb

12. Ⓐ join in on the chorus
    Ⓑ a game of checkers
    Ⓒ the piano keyboard
    Ⓓ climed into bed

13. Ⓐ the kikball team
    Ⓑ roll up the carpet
    Ⓒ numb fingers and toes
    Ⓓ a clever student

14. Ⓐ knuckle of my finger
    Ⓑ my favorite charikter
    Ⓒ the brass knob on the door
    Ⓓ a snack of crackers

15. Ⓐ kneel down by the baby
    Ⓑ a poisonous chemical
    Ⓒ comb his hair
    Ⓓ cheese and krackers

16. Ⓐ a tale of a knight
    Ⓑ voices began to echo
    Ⓒ komb your hair
    Ⓓ hit my knuckle

17. Ⓐ a nail or a thumbtack
    Ⓑ a game of chekurs
    Ⓒ clothing design
    Ⓓ knowledge to share

18. Ⓐ tradition and kustom
    Ⓑ roll out the carpet
    Ⓒ a character sketch
    Ⓓ the hall closet

19. Ⓐ naw on her knuckles
    Ⓑ rattle the knob
    Ⓒ read about a gnome
    Ⓓ play checkers or chess

20. Ⓐ a tree with gnarled limbs
    Ⓑ a typewriter keyboard
    Ⓒ her mom's favorite kookbook
    Ⓓ a biting gnat

21. Ⓐ a package of crackers
    Ⓑ a clever question
    Ⓒ a kickball match
    Ⓓ the sword of the nite

22. Ⓐ gnaw through the rope
    Ⓑ an old custom
    Ⓒ break a lim
    Ⓓ to feel totally numb

23. Ⓐ freckles on his arms
    Ⓑ chemacal plant
    Ⓒ join in on the chorus
    Ⓓ climbed the ladder

24. Ⓐ the nob on the cupboard door
    Ⓑ the sharp point of a thumbtack
    Ⓒ design and build
    Ⓓ the keys on a keyboard

25. Ⓐ a repeated echo
    Ⓑ a clever reply
    Ⓒ wrote about a character
    Ⓓ dates on a kalendar

Read each group of words. Mark the circle next to the word that is misspelled.

1. Ⓐ moth
   Ⓑ howl
   Ⓒ pownd
   Ⓓ powerful

2. Ⓐ athleet
   Ⓑ somewhat
   Ⓒ thorough
   Ⓓ whiz

3. Ⓐ kounter
   Ⓑ whistle
   Ⓒ though
   Ⓓ drought

4. Ⓐ somewhat
   Ⓑ coward
   Ⓒ whatever
   Ⓓ cowch

5. Ⓐ downtown
   Ⓑ thril
   Ⓒ theater
   Ⓓ athlete

6. Ⓐ moth
   Ⓑ shower
   Ⓒ counter
   Ⓓ owch

7. Ⓐ thawrn
   Ⓑ howl
   Ⓒ powder
   Ⓓ couch

8. Ⓐ though
   Ⓑ whatever
   Ⓒ mownd
   Ⓓ downtown

9. Ⓐ drought
   Ⓑ bowgh
   Ⓒ bounce
   Ⓓ beneath

10. Ⓐ scout
    Ⓑ thorough
    Ⓒ whirlwind
    Ⓓ pouder

11. Ⓐ whiz
    Ⓑ threat
    Ⓒ thurteenth
    Ⓓ thrill

12. Ⓐ shouer
    Ⓑ whistle
    Ⓒ thorn
    Ⓓ athlete

13. Ⓐ ouch
    Ⓑ theeter
    Ⓒ somewhat
    Ⓓ coward

14. Ⓐ couch
    Ⓑ downtown
    Ⓒ bounse
    Ⓓ counter

15. Ⓐ beneath
    Ⓑ bough
    Ⓒ werlwind
    Ⓓ thrill

16. Ⓐ skout
    Ⓑ mound
    Ⓒ powerful
    Ⓓ whatever

17. Ⓐ though
    Ⓑ thret
    Ⓒ thirteenth
    Ⓓ whiz

18. Ⓐ thorough
    Ⓑ pound
    Ⓒ powder
    Ⓓ downtoun

19. Ⓐ whistles
    Ⓑ whatevur
    Ⓒ thorn
    Ⓓ shower

20. Ⓐ koward
    Ⓑ ouch
    Ⓒ howl
    Ⓓ bough

21. Ⓐ somewhat
    Ⓑ theater
    Ⓒ tho
    Ⓓ mound

22. Ⓐ whirlwind
    Ⓑ thirteenth
    Ⓒ bounce
    Ⓓ drowt

23. Ⓐ moth
    Ⓑ wistle
    Ⓒ scout
    Ⓓ threat

24. Ⓐ pound
    Ⓑ powerful
    Ⓒ coward
    Ⓓ beneeth

25. Ⓐ mawth
    Ⓑ bounce
    Ⓒ shower
    Ⓓ thorn

Read each group of words. Mark the circle next to the word that is spelled correctly.

1. Ⓐ mischeif
   Ⓑ mischief
   Ⓒ mischef
   Ⓓ mischeff

2. Ⓐ destrust
   Ⓑ distrist
   Ⓒ distrust
   Ⓓ disstrust

3. Ⓐ seize
   Ⓑ seise
   Ⓒ sieze
   Ⓓ seze

4. Ⓐ releif
   Ⓑ releef
   Ⓒ releaf
   Ⓓ relief

5. Ⓐ deslike
   Ⓑ dislik
   Ⓒ dislike
   Ⓓ deslik

6. Ⓐ recieve
   Ⓑ receive
   Ⓒ reseive
   Ⓓ resieve

7. Ⓐ unusuel
   Ⓑ unusule
   Ⓒ unusuil
   Ⓓ unusual

8. Ⓐ believe
   Ⓑ beleive
   Ⓒ beleve
   Ⓓ beleave

9. Ⓐ unfriendly
   Ⓑ unfreindly
   Ⓒ unfrendly
   Ⓓ unfrienly

10. Ⓐ reveiw
    Ⓑ revyou
    Ⓒ review
    Ⓓ revoo

11. Ⓐ desobey
    Ⓑ disobey
    Ⓒ disobay
    Ⓓ desobay

12. Ⓐ reendeer
    Ⓑ riendeer
    Ⓒ reindear
    Ⓓ reindeer

13. Ⓐ greif
    Ⓑ grief
    Ⓒ greef
    Ⓓ greaf

14. Ⓐ weigh
    Ⓑ wiegh
    Ⓒ waigh
    Ⓓ waegh

15. Ⓐ liesure
    Ⓑ leizure
    Ⓒ leisure
    Ⓓ leezure

16. Ⓐ unfoalded
    Ⓑ unfoulded
    Ⓒ unfolded
    Ⓓ unfoolded

17. Ⓐ cheef
    Ⓑ cheif
    Ⓒ cheaf
    Ⓓ chief

18. Ⓐ disagre
    Ⓑ disagree
    Ⓒ desagree
    Ⓓ disaggre

19. Ⓐ fierce
    Ⓑ feirce
    Ⓒ ierse
    Ⓓ feerce

20. Ⓐ disapere
    Ⓑ disappair
    Ⓒ disappear
    Ⓓ disappeer

21. Ⓐ vaile
    Ⓑ viel
    Ⓒ vael
    Ⓓ veil

22. Ⓐ unluckey
    Ⓑ unluky
    Ⓒ unluckie
    Ⓓ unlucky

23. Ⓐ niece
    Ⓑ neice
    Ⓒ neece
    Ⓓ neace

24. Ⓐ unsertain
    Ⓑ uncertain
    Ⓒ uncertan
    Ⓓ uncerten

25. Ⓐ cealing
    Ⓑ cieling
    Ⓒ ceiling
    Ⓓ ceeling

Read each sentence. Mark the circle to indicate the misspelled word. Mark circle D if there are no mistakes.

1. Ⓐ Ⓑ Ⓒ Ⓓ   Her stardom came as a result of a neighberhood fashion show.
       A   B   C

2. Ⓐ Ⓑ Ⓒ Ⓓ   In my opinion, he made a wise decision to join a fittness club.
       A   B   C

3. Ⓐ Ⓑ Ⓒ Ⓓ   Our nasion has a long tradition of freedom.
       A   B   C

4. Ⓐ Ⓑ Ⓒ Ⓓ   A serious childhood illness can cause parents great sadness.
                   A   B   C

5. Ⓐ Ⓑ Ⓒ Ⓓ   She wore an ekspression of kindness and tenderness.
                   A   B   C

6. Ⓐ Ⓑ Ⓒ Ⓓ   There is no question that I will read at least one ficshun book during my vacation.
                   A   B   C

7. Ⓐ Ⓑ Ⓒ Ⓓ   In addition to her goodness, she was also known for her wisdum.
                 A   B   C

Read each group of phrases. Mark the circle next to the phrase with the word that is misspelled.

8. Ⓐ voted for statehood
   Ⓑ protection of the witness
   Ⓒ Goodness me!
   Ⓓ an African kingdum

9. Ⓐ a school tradition
   Ⓑ his entire addulthood
   Ⓒ in fashion
   Ⓓ sorrow and sadness

10. Ⓐ fact or opiniun
    Ⓑ the freedom from fear
    Ⓒ the chicken's tenderness
    Ⓓ wished for stardom

11. Ⓐ Idaho's statehood
    Ⓑ answer my queschon
    Ⓒ a serious illness
    Ⓓ protection from the rain

12. Ⓐ a hasty decision
    Ⓑ a new nation
    Ⓒ adition and subtraction
    Ⓓ filled with wisdom

13. Ⓐ fact or fiction
    Ⓑ in my old neighborhood
    Ⓒ my first impreshon
    Ⓓ goodness to reply

14. Ⓐ the queen's kingdom
    Ⓑ a helpful suggestion
    Ⓒ addition problems
    Ⓓ the fight for freedum

15. Ⓐ a joyful occassion
    Ⓑ respect his opinion
    Ⓒ a question of luck
    Ⓓ health and fitness

16. Ⓐ great stardom
    Ⓑ spring vacasion
    Ⓒ a sad expression
    Ⓓ darkness fell

17. Ⓐ her own creation
    Ⓑ a neighborhood park
    Ⓒ a sad occasion
    Ⓓ anniversary of staethood

18. Ⓐ proud of his nation
    Ⓑ lightness and darkness
    Ⓒ all of his childhod
    Ⓓ a fashion magazine

19. Ⓐ offer him protektion
    Ⓑ reach adulthood
    Ⓒ a very bad impression
    Ⓓ known for his kindness

20. Ⓐ fiction and nonfiction
    Ⓑ an original creasion
    Ⓒ a suggestion box
    Ⓓ your opinion

21. Ⓐ a kind expression
    Ⓑ in darkness
    Ⓒ a deep saddness
    Ⓓ a happy occasion

22. Ⓐ the largest nation in Asia
    Ⓑ admired her wisdom
    Ⓒ responsibility of freedom
    Ⓓ out of fashan

23. Ⓐ a major dicision
    Ⓑ his first creation
    Ⓒ a very long illness
    Ⓓ an act of kindness

24. Ⓐ an important occasion
    Ⓑ an old tradition
    Ⓒ lasting impression
    Ⓓ scary darkniss

25. Ⓐ make a sugjestion
    Ⓑ a fitness magazine
    Ⓒ to rule the kingdom
    Ⓓ the summer vacation

Read each group of phrases. Mark the circle next to the phrase with the misspelled word.

1. Ⓐ peaches and cream
   Ⓑ allowed her to go
   Ⓒ were shown kindness
   Ⓓ cent a letter

2. Ⓐ piece of chicken
   Ⓑ mailboxs at the post office
   Ⓒ choose a partner
   Ⓓ waterproof matches

3. Ⓐ prefixs un- and dis-
   Ⓑ heard the question
   Ⓒ scent of flowers
   Ⓓ artist's sketches

4. Ⓐ patches of blue sky
   Ⓑ make quick sketches
   Ⓒ a heard of cattle
   Ⓓ think aloud

5. Ⓐ three bosses in one office
   Ⓑ rashes and bumps
   Ⓒ cost one sent
   Ⓓ stitches with thread

6. Ⓐ ham sandwitches
   Ⓑ a book of matches
   Ⓒ sent a package
   Ⓓ chews gum

7. Ⓐ empty the mailboxes
   Ⓑ chews a book to read
   Ⓒ threw a curve ball
   Ⓓ three guesses

8. Ⓐ no bikes allowed
   Ⓑ chews with his mouth closed
   Ⓒ piece of cake
   Ⓓ inchs in a foot

9. Ⓐ peace not war
   Ⓑ were shone to the door
   Ⓒ threw a fit
   Ⓓ peaches in the orchard

10. Ⓐ no smoking allowed
    Ⓑ knitting stitches
    Ⓒ sewed on the patchs
    Ⓓ sandwiches for lunch

11. Ⓐ slowly choose her food
    Ⓑ round up the herd
    Ⓒ read aloud
    Ⓓ matches up the socks

12. Ⓐ made two speechs
    Ⓑ dark and curly eyelashes
    Ⓒ adding prefixes
    Ⓓ not worth a cent

13. Ⓐ scent of suntan lotion
    Ⓑ mailboxes full of mail
    Ⓒ inches in length
    Ⓓ signed a piece treaty

14. Ⓐ bosses us around
    Ⓑ pick peachs
    Ⓒ choose a project
    Ⓓ a nickel and a cent

15. Ⓐ shone the flashlight
    Ⓑ sent a message
    Ⓒ through the Frisbee very high
    Ⓓ leather patches

16. Ⓐ heard a crash
    Ⓑ the wonderful cent of perfume
    Ⓒ long and boring speeches
    Ⓓ several batches of bread

17. Ⓐ sun shown in her eyes
    Ⓑ herd the sheep
    Ⓒ threw the pitch
    Ⓓ make wild guesses

18. Ⓐ ordered turkey sandwiches
    Ⓑ sent a bill
    Ⓒ fired by her bosses
    Ⓓ long eyelashez

19. Ⓐ a trail through the mountains
    Ⓑ chews slowly and carefully
    Ⓒ a peace of pie
    Ⓓ batches of cookie dough

20. Ⓐ a herd of goats
    Ⓑ two tennis matchs
    Ⓒ read aloud the letter
    Ⓓ mend with tiny stitches

21. Ⓐ itchy rashes
    Ⓑ listened to three speeches
    Ⓒ piece of paper
    Ⓓ path threw the forest

22. Ⓐ sketchs and paintings
    Ⓑ prefixes and suffixes
    Ⓒ peace of mind
    Ⓓ roast beef sandwiches

23. Ⓐ six inches wide
    Ⓑ movie was shown
    Ⓒ false eyelashes
    Ⓓ batchs of cookies

24. Ⓐ stars shone in the sky
    Ⓑ herd a noise
    Ⓒ diseases with rashes
    Ⓓ a tunnel through the mountain

25. Ⓐ no entry allowed
    Ⓑ choose to stay behind
    Ⓒ three gesses
    Ⓓ scent of a skunk

Read each group of words. Mark the circle next to the word that is misspelled.

1. Ⓐ hardware
   Ⓑ daisies
   Ⓒ bakground
   Ⓓ centuries

2. Ⓐ entries
   Ⓑ overboard
   Ⓒ melodies
   Ⓓ dutys

3. Ⓐ countrys
   Ⓑ splashdown
   Ⓒ victories
   Ⓓ mysteries

4. Ⓐ cities
   Ⓑ bullys
   Ⓒ daybreak
   Ⓓ worries

5. Ⓐ barefoot
   Ⓑ copys
   Ⓒ toothpick
   Ⓓ cloudburst

6. Ⓐ schoolyard
   Ⓑ melodies
   Ⓒ headake
   Ⓓ laundries

7. Ⓐ strawberries
   Ⓑ seashore
   Ⓒ daybreak
   Ⓓ daisys

8. Ⓐ entrys
   Ⓑ cloudburst
   Ⓒ hummingbird
   Ⓓ victories

9. Ⓐ centurys
   Ⓑ overboard
   Ⓒ batteries
   Ⓓ countries

10. Ⓐ headache
    Ⓑ gentelmen
    Ⓒ runaway
    Ⓓ teammate

11. Ⓐ cities
    Ⓑ background
    Ⓒ splashdown
    Ⓓ hardwear

12. Ⓐ melodies
    Ⓑ toothpick
    Ⓒ skoolyard
    Ⓓ laundries

13. Ⓐ duties
    Ⓑ mysterys
    Ⓒ bullies
    Ⓓ gentlemen

14. Ⓐ copies
    Ⓑ worrys
    Ⓒ daisies
    Ⓓ seashore

15. Ⓐ victories
    Ⓑ strawberries
    Ⓒ citys
    Ⓓ daybreak

16. Ⓐ countries
    Ⓑ batteries
    Ⓒ laundries
    Ⓓ humingbird

17. Ⓐ victorys
    Ⓑ barefoot
    Ⓒ runaway
    Ⓓ teammate

18. Ⓐ worries
    Ⓑ copies
    Ⓒ strawberrys
    Ⓓ entries

19. Ⓐ gentlemen
    Ⓑ mysteries
    Ⓒ background
    Ⓓ melodys

20. Ⓐ batteries
    Ⓑ laundrys
    Ⓒ splashdown
    Ⓓ daisies

21. Ⓐ cloudberst
    Ⓑ hardware
    Ⓒ centuries
    Ⓓ hummingbird

22. Ⓐ overboard
    Ⓑ cities
    Ⓒ teemmate
    Ⓓ schoolyard

23. Ⓐ countries
    Ⓑ entries
    Ⓒ gentlemen
    Ⓓ seeshore

24. Ⓐ bearfoot
    Ⓑ toothpick
    Ⓒ bullies
    Ⓓ runaway

25. Ⓐ headache
    Ⓑ batterys
    Ⓒ duties
    Ⓓ centuries

Read each sentence. Mark the circle to indicate the misspelled word. Mark circle D if there are no mistakes.

1. Ⓐ Ⓑ Ⓒ Ⓓ   She made <u>scarfs</u> from old <u>handkerchiefs</u> and <u>jerseys</u>.
                              A   B   C

2. Ⓐ Ⓑ Ⓒ Ⓓ   The <u>thieves</u> used <u>knives</u> to open the <u>saves</u>.
                          A   B   C

3. Ⓐ Ⓑ Ⓒ Ⓓ   <u>Wolves</u> come down to the <u>vallies</u> to attack the young <u>calves</u>.
                      A   B   C

4. Ⓐ Ⓑ Ⓒ Ⓓ   The <u>guys</u> on the oil rig looked forward to seeing their <u>wifes</u> during the <u>holidays</u>.
                          A   B   C

5. Ⓐ Ⓑ Ⓒ Ⓓ   Most <u>monkeys</u> live longer <u>lives</u> than <u>turkeys</u>.
                            A   B   C

6. Ⓐ Ⓑ Ⓒ Ⓓ   Put the <u>loaves</u> of bread on <u>trays</u> on these <u>shelfs</u>.
                            A   B   C

7. Ⓐ Ⓑ Ⓒ Ⓓ   Riding the <u>donkys</u> on paved <u>highways</u> will hurt their <u>hooves</u>.
                              A   B   C

Read each group of words. Mark the circle next to the word that is misspelled.

8. Ⓐ thieves Ⓑ jerseys Ⓒ halways Ⓓ calves	14. Ⓐ guys Ⓑ calfs Ⓒ weekdays Ⓓ turkeys	20. Ⓐ handkercheves Ⓑ cuffs Ⓒ donkeys Ⓓ holidays
9. Ⓐ wolvs Ⓑ valleys Ⓒ surveys Ⓓ knives	15. Ⓐ loaves Ⓑ decoys Ⓒ thiefs Ⓓ hallways	21. Ⓐ knives Ⓑ monkeys Ⓒ chimneys Ⓓ hoovs
10. Ⓐ hooves Ⓑ dissplays Ⓒ holidays Ⓓ scarves	16. Ⓐ halves Ⓑ monkys Ⓒ lives Ⓓ wolves	22. Ⓐ displays Ⓑ hallways Ⓒ highways Ⓓ weakdays
11. Ⓐ turkeys Ⓑ cuffs Ⓒ weekdays Ⓓ hiways	17. Ⓐ handkerchiefs Ⓑ scarves Ⓒ safes Ⓓ jerzeys	23. Ⓐ valleys Ⓑ looves Ⓒ halves Ⓓ wolves
12. Ⓐ safes Ⓑ chiefs Ⓒ donkeys Ⓓ halfs	18. Ⓐ wives Ⓑ chimneys Ⓒ nives Ⓓ shelves	24. Ⓐ holidazes Ⓑ shelves Ⓒ wives Ⓓ decoys
13. Ⓐ chiminys Ⓑ decoys Ⓒ cuffs Ⓓ chiefs	19. Ⓐ lives Ⓑ trazs Ⓒ guys Ⓓ surveys	25. Ⓐ displays Ⓑ surveys Ⓒ cheifs Ⓓ trays

Answer Key for Student Edition Lessons

Lesson 1 Words With Long *a* and Long *e*
Pages 2–5

Write the Words

Order of answers may vary.

1. bacon, flavor, statement, chase, stains, afraid
2. recent, even, treat, please, breathe, these, complete, greedy, wheels

Spelling and Language

1. treat 2. breathe 3. please 4. flavor 5. complete
6. stains 7. recent 8. greedy 9. wheels 10. afraid 11. these
12. chase 13. bacon 14. statement 15. even

Build Vocabulary/ Real-Life Spelling

1. chase 2. complete 3. even 4. wheels 5. statement
6. these 7. breathe 8. stains 9. recent 10. afraid
11. please 12. flavor 13. bacon 14. treat 15. bacon
16. flavor 17. please 18. treat 19. greedy

Spelling Review

Riddle answer: bacon

Lesson 2 Words With Long *i* and Long *o*
Pages 6–9

Write the Words

Order of answers may vary.

1. pirate, silence, spider, iceberg, spine, lifetime, highest, fright
2. hotel, odor, elbow, below, coast, smoke, globe

Spelling and Language

1. pirate 2. spider 3. iceberg 4. lifetime 5. hotel 6. elbow
7. spine 8. fright 9. coast 10. smoke 11. globe 12. odor
13. silence 14. highest 15. below

Build Vocabulary/ Real-Life Spelling

1. elbow 2. globe 3. silence 4. coast 5. iceberg 6. spine
7. below 8. hotel 9. odor 10. fright 11. spider
12. highest 13. smoke 14. lifetime 15. pirate 16. pirate
17. coast 18. fright 19. spine 20. lifetime

Spelling Review

1. below 2. coast 3. elbow 4. fright 5. globe 6. highest
7. hotel 8. iceberg 9. lifetime 10. odor 11. pirate
12. silence 13. smoke 14. spider 15. spine

Lesson 3 Words With /l/
Pages 10–13

Write the Words

Order of answers may vary.

1. spiral, loyal, mammal 2. gravel, shovel, nickel 3. pencil, April 4. middle, tickle, sparkle, crumble, huddle, sniffle, bubble

Spelling and Language

1. crumble 2. pencil 3. shovel 4. loyal 5. April 6. sniffle
7. bubble 8. nickel 9. spiral 10. tickle 11. sparkle
12. mammal 13. middle 14. gravel 15. huddle 16. spiral
17. gravel 18. bubble 19. sparkle 20. tickle

Build Vocabulary/ Real-Life Spelling

1. nickel 2. April 3. shovel 4. mammal 5. bubble
6. sniffle 7. gravel 8. crumble 9. loyal 10. tickle 11. huddle
12. pencil 13. sparkle 14. spiral 15. pencil 16. middle
17. sparkle

Spelling Review

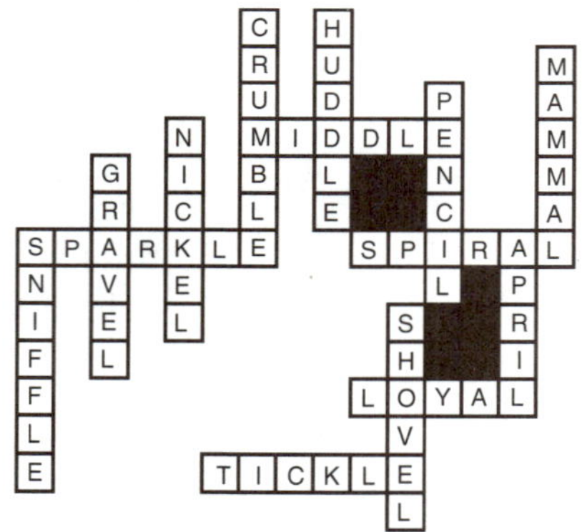

Riddle answer: bubble

Lesson 4 Words With Short *e* and Short *u*
Pages 14–17

Write the Words

Order of answers may vary.

1. friendship, pleasant, leather, healthy, steady, breath, spread 2. southern, wonderful, tongue, twist, touched, month, bunch, other

Spelling and Language

1. breath 2. month 3. bunch 4. spread 5. trust 6. tongue
7. healthy 8. friendship 9. wonderful 10. southern
11. pleasant 12. steady 13. touched 14. leather 15. other
16. healthy 17. breath

Build Vocabulary/ Real-Life Spelling

1. tongue 2. month 3. wonderful 4. leather 5. southern
6. healthy 7. touched 8. steady 9. trust 10. bunch
11. spread 12. breath 13. pleasant 14. wonderful
15. month 16. bunch 17. other 18. leather

Spelling Review

Lesson 5 Words Ending With *-ing*
Pages 18–21

Write the Words

Order of answers may vary.

1. speeding, cheating, spending, spilling, training, twisting,
catching, teaching 2. bothering, suggesting, gathering,
ordering, opening, directing, borrowing

Spelling and Language

1. suggesting 2. borrowing 3. speeding 4. spending
5. twisting 6. directing 7. teaching 8. bothering 9. ordering
10. catching 11. training 12. spilling 13. opening
14. training 15. gathering 16. cheating 17. opening

Build Vocabulary/ Real-Life Spelling

1. directing 2. training 3. bothering 4. borrowing
5. ordering 6. spending 7. speeding 8. spilling 9. cheating
10. opening 11. gathering 12. twisting 13. suggesting
14. teaching 15. catching 16. spending 17. gathering
18. teaching 19. ordering 20. catching

Spelling Review

1. TEACHING
2. GATHERING
3. CHEATING
4. OPENING
5. SPILLING
6. DIRECTING
7. BOTHERING
8. TRAINING
9. SPEEDING

10. SPENDING
11. TWISTING
12. SUGGESTING
13. BORROWING
14. CATCHING
15. ORDERING

Riddle answer: a railroad engine

Lesson 6 Adjectives Ending in *-y*
Pages 22–25

Write the Words

Order of answers may vary.

1. sandy, itchy, filthy, salty 2. wavy, shaky, lacy, scaly,
smoky, bony, wrinkly, breezy 3. starry, foggy, stubby

Spelling and Language

1. foggy 2. breezy 3. sandy 4. scaly 5. stubby 6. itchy
7. smoky 8. wrinkly 9. salty 10. bony 11. filthy 12. wavy
13. starry 14. shaky 15. lacy 16. wavy 17. sandy
18. wrinkly 19. foggy 20. bony

Build Vocabulary/ Real-Life Spelling

1. breezy 2. filthy 3. wrinkly 4. shaky 5. smoky 6. bony
7. stubby 8. lacy 9. wavy 10. itchy 11. foggy 12. sandy
13. starry 14. salty 15. scaly 16. sandy 17. salty
18. scaly 19. itchy 20. foggy 21. starry

Spelling Review

Order of answers may vary. Allow for some overlapping.

1. Sight: filthy, stubby, lacy, wavy, foggy, starry 2. Taste:
salty 3. Smell: smoky 4. Touch: wrinkly, shaky, bony,
sandy, scaly, itchy, breezy

Lesson 7 More About Adding *-ing*
Pages 26–29

Write the Words

Order of answers may vary.

1. splitting, gripping, plotting, shipping, bragging, slapping,
occurring
2. admitting, beginning, throbbing, permitting, preferring,
outrunning, upsetting, forgetting

Spelling and Language

1. forgetting 2. outrunning 3. permitting 4. admitting
5. bragging 6. preferring 7. upsetting 8. beginning
9. splitting 10. slapping 11. occurring 12. snipping
13. plotting 14. throbbing 15, 16. gripping, snipping
17, 18, 19. splitting, admitting, permitting

Build Vocabulary/ Real-Life Spelling

1. admitting 2. permitting 3. preferring 4. beginning
5. bragging 6. upsetting 7. forgetting 8. slapping
9. outrunning 10. throbbing 11. splitting 12. gripping
13. plotting 14. occurring 15. snipping 16. throbbing
17. splitting 18. upsetting 19. beginning 20. admitting

Spelling Review

1. preferring 2. outrunning 3. beginning 4. upsetting
5. permitting 6. bragging 7. admitting 8. splitting
9. forgetting 10. gripping 11. throbbing 12. snipping
13. slapping 14. occurring 15. plotting

Lesson 8 Contractions
Pages 30–33

Write the Words

Order of answers may vary.

1. he'll, she'll 2. who'd 3. they've, we've 4. wasn't, won't,
couldn't, can't, doesn't, don't, weren't, isn't, hasn't, aren't

Spelling and Language

1. we've 2. he'll 3. they've 4. she'll 5. who'd 6. aren't
7. wasn't 8. doesn't 9. won't 10. couldn't 11. can't
12. weren't 13. hasn't 14. isn't 15. don't 16. aren't
17. isn't 18. don't 19. can't

Build Vocabulary/ Real-Life Spelling

1. aren't 2. wasn't 3. she'll 4. weren't 5. isn't 6. hasn't
7. who'd 8. can't 9. won't 10. doesn't 11. he'll
12. weren't 13. couldn't 14. don't 15. we've 16. they've
17. we've 18. couldn't 19. he'll

Spelling Review

1. he'll 2. can't 3. isn't 4. who'd 5. won't 6. aren't
7. wasn't 8 couldn't 9. we've 10. doesn't 11. hasn't
12. weren't 13. don't 14. they've 15. she'll

Lesson 9 Words With /s/
Pages 34–37

Write the Words

Order of answers may vary.

1. insult, ancestor, person, suitcase 2. descend, scissors,
science, muscle 3. across, progress, harmless, grassy
4. icicle, advice, ancestor, cereal, science

Spelling and Language

1. suitcase 2. science 3. muscle 4. icicle 5. cereal
6. ancestor 7. insult 8. person 9. descend 10. progress
11. grassy 12. harmless 13. advice 14. scissors
15. across 16. science 17. muscle

Build Vocabulary/ Real-Life Spelling

1. cereal 2. grassy 3. scissors 4. icicle 5. suitcase
6. science 7. muscle 8. ancestor 9. descend 10. insult
11. advice 12. across 13. person 14. progress 15. harmless
16. advice 17. person 18. across 19. progress
20. harmless

Spelling Review

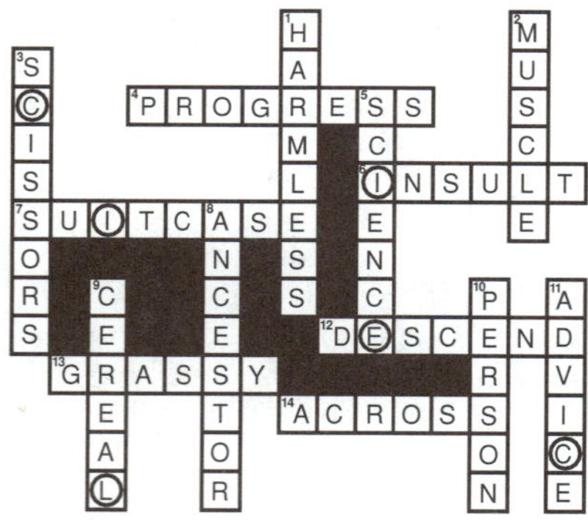

Riddle Answer: icicle

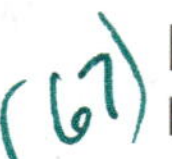

Lesson 10 Irregular Verbs
Pages 38–41

Write the Words

Order of answers may vary.

1. bought, thought, fought, brought 2. taught, caught
3. slept, crept 4. built 5. spoke, chose, wrote, stole, broke,
tore

Spelling and Language

1. thought 2. taught 3. fought 4. stole 5. caught 6. wrote
7. chose 8. crept 9. tore 10. slept 11. spoke 12. bought
13. brought 14. bought 15. broke 16. brought 17. built

Build Vocabulary/ Real-Life Spelling

1. taught 2. chose 3. slept 4. built 5. stole 6. wrote
7. fought 8. crept 9. bought 10. spoke 11. thought
12. caught 13. brought 14. broke 15. tore 16. caught
17. broke 18. tore 19. brought 20. chose

Spelling Review

Lesson 11 Words With /z/
Pages 42–45

Write the Words

Order of answers may vary.

1. freeze, zebra, zigzag, lizard 2. jazz, buzzer
3. supposed, lose, clothes, present, packages, dinners,
refuse, advise 4. xylophone

Spelling and Language

1. zebra 2. present 3. lizard 4. xylophone 5. buzzer
6. dinner 7. freeze 8. jazz 9. advise 10. zigzag
11. supposed 12. clothes 13. refuse, lose 14. present
15. dinners 16. lizard 17. packages

Build Vocabulary/Real-Life Spelling

1. lose 2. clothes 3. dinners 4. supposed 5. zigzag
6. freeze 7. lizard 8. zebra 9. refuse 10. advise 11. present
12. buzzer 13. packages 14. dinners 15. jazz
16. xylophone 17. clothes 18. present

Spelling Review

1. advise 2. buzzer 3. clothes 4. dinners 5. freeze
6. jazz 7. lizard 8. lose 9. packages 10. present 11. refuse
12. supposed 13. xylophone 14. zebra 15. zigzag

Lesson 12 Adding *-er* and *-est*
Pages 46–49

Write the Words

Order of answers may vary.

1. sillier, silliest, wealthier, wealthiest, fancier, fanciest
2. looser, loosest, larger, largest, strangest
3. hotter, hottest, madder, maddest

Spelling and Language

1. sillier 2. hotter 3. loosest 4. fanciest 5. strangest
6. silliest 7. madder 8. largest 9. maddest 10. wealthiest
11. larger 12. wealthier 13. looser 14. hottest 15. fancier
16. fancier 17. silliest 18. larger 19. wealthiest
20. hottest 21. loosest 22. strangest 23. madder

Build Vocabulary/ Real-Life Spelling

1. maddest 2. strangest 3. sillier 4. hottest 5. larger
6. fancier 7. hotter 8. fanciest 9. silliest 10. largest
11. madder 12. loosest 13. wealthier 14. wealthiest
15. looser

Spelling Review

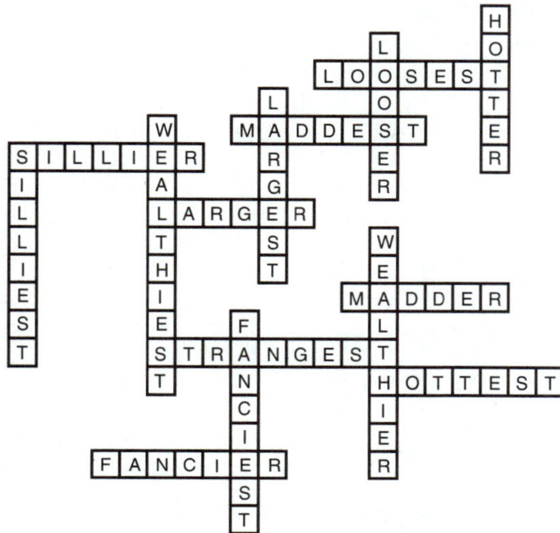

Lesson 13 Words With Silent Letters
Pages 50–53

Write the Words

Order of answers may vary.

1. knob, kneel, knight, knuckle, knowledge
2. comb, numb, limb, climbed, thumbtack
3. gnat, gnaw, gnarled, gnome, design

Spelling and Language

1. gnat 2. comb 3. knob 4. thumbtack 5. knight
6. gnome 7. limb 8. limb 9. climbed 10. gnarled
11. knowledge 12. gnaw 13. knob 14. knight
15. thumbtack 16. kneel 17. knuckle 18. numb
19. design 20. gnat 21. gnome, comb

Build Vocabulary/ Real-Life Spelling

1. knob 2. thumbtack 3. comb 4. knuckle 5. gnaw
6. climbed 7. numb 8. limb 9. kneel 10. gnarled 11. knight
12. gnome 13. gnat 14. design 15. design 16. knight
17. gnome 18. gnat 19. knowledge

Spelling Review

Answer to question: knob

Lesson 14 Words With /k/
Pages 54–57

Write the Words

Order of answers may vary.

1. clever, calendar, closet, custom, carpet, cookbook,
chemical, crackers, character 2. cookbook, keyboard,
kickball 3. checkers, kickball, freckles, crackers 4. echo,
chemical, character, chorus

Spelling and Language

1. chemical 2. carpet 3. closet 4. freckles 5. crackers
6. kickball 7. chorus 8. echo 9. character 10. custom
11. clever 12. calendar 13. checkers 14. carpet
15. chemical 16. echo 17. keyboard 18. cookbook
19. closet 20. crackers 21. chorus

Build Vocabulary/ Real-Life Spelling

1. custom 2. clever 3. echo 4. freckles 5. chemical
6. crackers 7. character 8. closet 9. keyboard 10. calendar
11. kickball 12. chorus 13. carpet 14. cookbook
15. checkers 16. keyboard 17. cookbook 18. calendar
19. character 20. closet

Spelling Review

1. calendar 2. carpet 3. character 4. checkers 5. chemical
6. chorus 7. clever 8. closet 9. cookbook 10. crackers
11. custom 12. echo 13. freckles 14. keyboard 15. kickball

Lesson 15 Words With /ou/
Pages 58–61

Write the Words

Order of answers may vary.

1. ouch, bounce, pound, counter, couch, mound, scout
2. powder, shower, coward, howl, powerful, downtown
3. bough, drought

Spelling and Language

1. howl 2. bough 3. bounce 4. powder 5. coward
6. shower 7. scout, drought 8. couch, ouch 9. mound,
pound 10. coward 11. counter 12. powder 13. shower
14. scout 15. pound 16. couch 17. mound 18. howl
19. downtown 20. ouch 21. coward 22. scout 23. mound
24. shower 25. bough

Build Vocabulary/ Real-Life Spelling

1. downtown 2. howl 3. bough 4. drought 5. powerful
6. bounce 7. counter 8. ouch 9. pound 10. coward
11. mound 12. powder 13. shower 14. couch 15. scout
16. powerful 17. drought 18. coward 19. scout 20. couch

Spelling Review

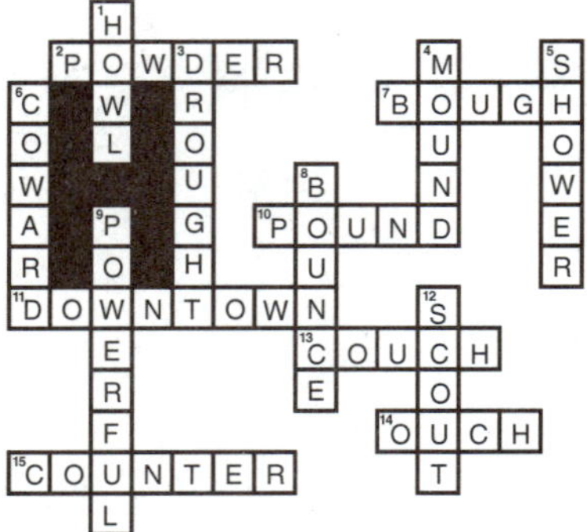

Lesson 16 Words With *wh* and *th*
Pages 62–65

Write the Words

Order of answers may vary.

1. whiz, whistle, whatever, whirlwind, somewhat
2. moth, threat, thorn, thrill, athlete, beneath, though, thorough, theater, thirteenth

Spelling and Language

1. athlete 2. whiz 3. theater 4. thorn 5. threat 6. though
7. threat 8. whisper 9. moth 10. thrill 11. thorough
12. whatever 13. thirteenth 14. thorough 15. beneath
16. somewhat 17. though 18. thorn 19. threat
20. whistle 21. athlete 22. thrill 23. whirlwind 24. theater
25. moth 26. whiz

Build Vocabulary/ Real-Life Spelling

1. whistle 2. moth 3. thorn 4. thirteenth 5. athlete
6. whirlwind 7. whiz 8. somewhat 9. whatever 10. beneath
11. thorough 12. theater 13. though 14. threat 15. thrill
16. though 17. thorough 18. thorough 19. though
20. though

Spelling Review

Lesson 17 Words With *ie* and *ei*
Pages 66–69

Write the Words

Order of answers may vary.

1. believe, chief, relief, grief, niece, fierce, review, mischief
2. receive, ceiling, leisure, seize, reindeer, veil, weigh

Spelling and Language

1. ceiling 2. review 3. chief, grief, relief 4. leisure 5. fierce
6. veil 7. niece 8. believe 9. weigh 10. receive 11. seize
12. relief 13. grief 14. reindeer 15. veil 16. chief
17. mischief 18. review 19. ceiling

Build Vocabulary/ Real-Life Spelling

1. niece 2. reindeer 3. believe 4. weigh 5. leisure
6. mischief 7. relief 8. seize 9. veil 10. ceiling
11. receive 12. chief 13. fierce 14. review 15. grief
16. fierce 17. grief 18. review 19. relief

Spelling Review

1. mischief 2. leisure 3. weigh 4. believe 5. niece
6. receive 7. veil 8. ceiling 9. chief 10. reindeer
11. fierce 12. seize 13. grief 14. review 15. relief

Lesson 18 Prefixes *dis-* and *un-*
Pages 70–73

Write the Words

Order of answers may vary.

1. dislike, disobey, disappear, distrust, disagree, discover
2. unlucky, unfriendly, unable, unusual, uncertain, unkind, unlock, unfolded, unpack

Spelling and Language

1. discover 2. unfriendly 3. unlock 4. distrust 5. unable
6. unfolded 7. dislike 8. uncertain 9. disagree
10. unpack 11. disappear 12. disobey 13. unlucky
14. unusual 15. unkind 16. unkind 17. unlock 18. dislike
19. disobey 20. unable 21. discover 22. unpack
23. disagree 24. unlock 25. disobey 26. dislike

Build Vocabulary/ Real-Life Spelling

1. unlucky 2. discover 3. unfriendly 4. disobey 5. unkind
6. unable 7. disagree 8. unlock 9. uncertain 10. dislike
11. unfolded 12. distrust 13. unpack 14. unusual
15. disappear 16. unusual 17. disappear 18. uncertain
19. unfriendly 20. discover

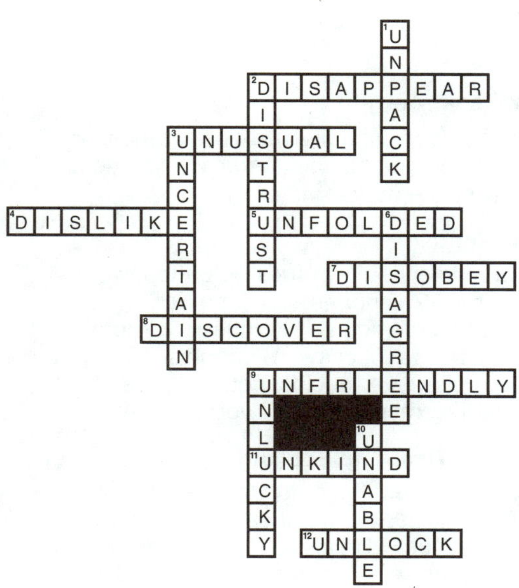

Lesson 19 Suffixes *-ness*, *-hood*, and *-dom*
Pages 74–77

Write the Words

Order of answers may vary.

1. kindness, sadness, illness, darkness, fitness, tenderness, goodness
2. neighborhood, childhood, adulthood, statehood
3. freedom, kingdom, stardom, wisdom

Spelling and Language

1. tenderness 2. kindness 3. stardom 4. statehood
5. goodness 6. darkness 7. neighborhood 8. wisdom
9. kingdom 10. fitness 11. sadness 12. childhood
13. adulthood 14. freedom 15. illness 16. fitness
17. sadness 18. illness 19. darkness 20. tenderness
21. sadness 22. kindness 23. stardom 24. fitness
25. darkness

Build Vocabulary/ Real-Life Spelling

1. tenderness 2. freedom 3. wisdom 4. darkness
5. kindness 6. childhood 7. kingdom 8. stardom
9. statehood 10. fitness 11. neighborhood 12. goodness
13. illness 14. childhood 15. wisdom 16. adulthood

Spelling Review

1. kindness 2. childhood 3. statehood 4. fitness
5. freedom 6. sadness 7. stardom 8. goodness
9. tenderness 10. wisdom 11. darkness 12. adulthood
13. neighborhood 14. kingdom 15. illness

Lesson 20 Words Ending With *-ion*
Pages 78–81

Write the Words

Order of answers may vary.

1. fashion 2. opinion 3. nation, fiction, vacation, question, addition, protection, suggestion, tradition, creation
4. decision, occasion 5. impression, expression

Spelling and Language

1. protection 2. suggestion 3. creation 4. decision
5. impression 6. expression 7. suggestion 8. opinion
9. question 10. nation 11. fiction 12. occasion 13. fiction
14. creation 15. tradition 16. fashion 17. addition
18. impression 19. nation 20. vacation

Build Vocabulary/ Real-Life Spelling

1. addition 2. fiction 3. vacation 4. creation 5. question
6. opinion 7. decision 8. expression 9. impression
10. tradition 11.suggestion 12. nation 13. fashion
14. occasion 15. protection 16. fashion 17. vacation
18. occasion 19. protection 20. question

Spelling Review

1. NATION
2. QUESTION
3. SUGGESTION
4. CREATION
5. DECISION
6. FICTION
7. TRADITION
8. OCCASION
9. OPINION
10. VACATION
11. FASHION
12. PROTECTION
13. ADDITION
14. IMPRESSION
15. EXPRESSION

Riddle answer: a question of time

Lesson 21 Homophones
Pages 82–85

Write the Words

Order of answers may vary.

1. sent, cent, scent 2. threw, through, chews, choose
3. herd, heard 4. aloud, allowed 5. peace, piece, shone, shown

Spelling and Language

1. peace 2. herd 3. scent 4. piece 5. choose 6. cent
7. shone 8. threw 9. heard 10. sent 11. through, threw
12. chews, choose 13. shown, shone 14. peace, piece
15. aloud, allowed 16. herd, heard 17. sent, cent, scent

Build Vocabulary/ Real-Life Spelling

1. cent 2. aloud 3. threw 4. shone 5. choose 6. sent
7. heard 8. allowed 9. chews 10. through 11. shown
12. herd 13. piece 14. peace 15. scent 16. peace
17. herd 18. scent 19. piece

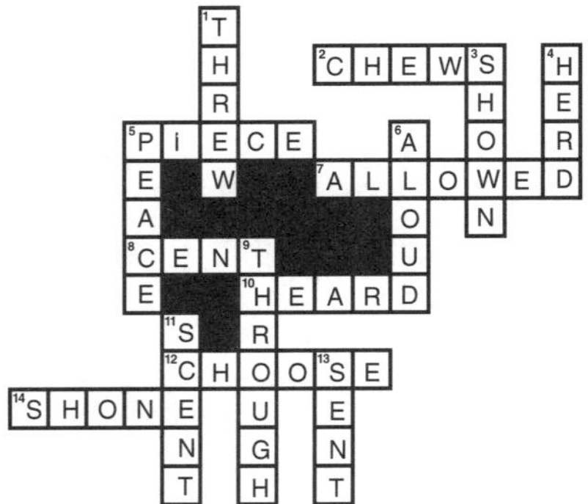

Lesson 22 Plural Nouns With *-es*
Pages 86–89

Write the Words

Order of answers may vary.

1. speeches, sandwiches, stitches, inches, sketches, matches, peaches, patches, batches 2. eyelashes, rashes 3. mailboxes, prefixes 4. guesses, bosses

Spelling and Language

1. guesses, bosses 2. prefixes, mailboxes 3. eyelashes, rashes 4. speeches 5. sandwiches 6. stitches 7. inches 8. sketches 9. matches 10. peaches 11. patches 12. batches 13. guesses 14. stitches 15. prefixes 16. eyelashes 17. sketches 18. peaches

Build Vocabulary/ Real-Life Spelling

1. matches 2. prefixes 3. sandwiches 4. peaches 5. patches 6. eyelashes 7. speeches 8. sketches 9. inches 10. guesses 11. batches 12. mailboxes 13. stitches 14. bosses 15. rashes 16. matches 17. bosses

Spelling Review

The missing study word is bosses.

Lesson 23 Forming Plural Nouns with *-ies*
Pages 90–93

Write the Words

Order of answers may vary.

1. cities, countries, copies, bullies, duties, worries, laundries, daisies, entries 2. strawberries, mysteries, melodies, batteries, centuries, victories

Spelling and Language

1. countries 2. mysteries 3. worries 4. batteries 5. bullies 6. daisies 7. laundries 8. centuries 9. cities 10. strawberries 11. melodies 12. duties 13. victories 14. copies 15. entries 16. cities 17. copies 18. mysteries 19. worries 20. bullies 21. copies, countries 22. daisies, duties 23. melodies, mysteries 24. worries

Build Vocabulary/ Real-Life Spelling

1. strawberries 2. bullies 3. countries 4. entries 5. laundries 6. mysteries 7. victories 8. batteries 9. centuries 10. duties 11. daisies 12. worries 13. cities 14. melodies 15. copies 16. cities 17. centuries 18. countries 19. batteries 20. duties 21. melodies 22. copies 23. mysteries

Spelling Review

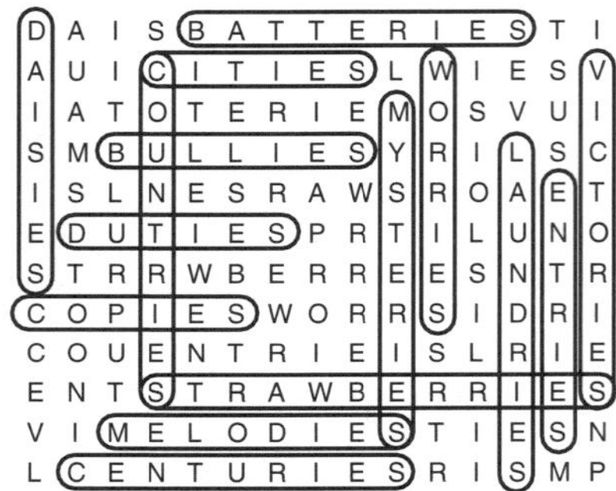

Lesson 24 Compound Words
Pages 94–97

Write the Words

Order of answers may vary.

1. background, barefoot, cloudburst, daybreak, gentlemen 2. hardware, headache, hummingbird, overboard, runaway 3. schoolyard, seashore, splashdown, teammate, toothpick

Spelling and Language

1. headache 2. hummingbird 3. teammate 4. overboard 5. background 6. daybreak 7. toothpick 8. cloudburst 9. runaway 10. gentlemen 11. schoolyard 12. seashore 13. barefoot 14. splashdown 15. hardware 16. cloudburst 17. daybreak 18. barefoot 19. hardware 20. schoolyard

Build Vocabulary/ Real-Life Spelling

1. seashore 2. splashdown 3. daybreak 4. schoolyard 5. hummingbird 6. overboard 7. gentlemen 8. cloudburst 9. hardware 10. runaway 11. background 12. toothpick 13. teammate 14. headache 15. barefoot 16. hummingbird 17. headache 18. barefoot 19. toothpick 20. seashore

Lesson 25 Plural Nouns Ending With *s*
Pages 98–101

Write the Words

Order of answers may vary.

1. trays, hallways, highways, displays, weekdays, holidays
2. donkeys, valleys, turkeys, surveys, monkeys, jerseys, chimneys
3. decoys, guys

Spelling and Language

1. turkeys 2. displays 3. decoys 4. trays 5. donkeys
6. monkeys 7. hallways 8. guys 9. chimneys
10. weekdays 11. jerseys 12. surveys 13. holidays
14. valleys 15. weekdays 16. hallways 17. highways
18. trays 19. hallways 20. monkeys 21. donkeys

Build Vocabulary/ Real-Life Spelling

1. chimneys 2. decoys 3. donkeys 4. turkeys 5. jerseys
6. trays 7. monkeys 8. guys 9. weekdays 10. surveys
11. valleys 12. highways 13. displays 14. hallways
15. holidays

Spelling Review

Lesson 26 Plural Nouns With *f/fe* words
Pages 102–105

Write the Words

Order of answers may vary.

1. wolves, scarves, calves, wives, lives, thieves, knives, halves, hooves, loaves, shelves
2. cuffs, chiefs, handkerchiefs
3. safes

Spelling and Language

1. shelves 2. chiefs 3. lives 4. calves 5. loaves 6. scarves
7. wolves 8. wives 9. hooves 10. thieves 11. knives
12. safes 13. halves 14. cuffs 15. handkerchiefs
16. thieves 17. hooves 18. shelves 19. loaves 20. cuffs
21. chiefs, handkerchiefs 22. knives, wives, lives 23. loaves
24. wolves 25. chiefs 26. wives

Build Vocabulary/ Real-Life Spelling

1. hooves 2. knives 3. thieves 4. handkerchiefs 5. loaves
6. lives 7. halves 8. cuffs 9. scarves 10. wives 11. wolves
12. safes 13. calves 14. chiefs 15. shelves 16. loaves
17. halves 18. shelves 19. hooves   20. scarves

Spelling Review

1. calves 2. chiefs 3. cuffs 4. halves 5. handkerchiefs
6. hooves 7. knives 8. lives 9. loaves 10. safes 11. scarves
12. shelves 13. thieves 14. wives 15. wolves

Spelling Test 1, page 7

1. C 2. A 3. B 4. D 5. C 6. D 7. B 8. A 9. D 10. B
11. C 12. A 13. C 14. B 15. B 16. A 17. D 18. C 19. D
20. A 21. A 22. B 23. D 24. C 25. B

Spelling Test 2, page 8

1. B 2. C 3. A 4. D 5. C 6. A 7. B 8. D 9. B 10. A 11. C
12. B 13. A 14. D 15. C 16. D 17. A 18. A 19. B 20. C
21. D 22. B 23. C 24. D 25. A

Spelling Test 3, page 9

1. B 2. A 3. D 4. C 5. A 6. B 7. D 8. C 9. C 10. A 11. D
12. A 13. D 14. B 15. D 16. B 17. C 18. B 19. A 20. C
21. D 22. B 23. C 24. A 25. B

Spelling Test 4, page 10

1. C 2. A 3. B 4. D 5. D 6. A 7. B 8. C 9. D 10. B 11. A
12. B 13. A 14. A 15. C 16. D 17. A 18. B 19. D 20. C
21. C 22. A 23. D 24. B 25. C

Spelling Test 5, page 11

1. B 2. D 3. A 4. C 5. A 6. C 7. D 8. B 9. B 10. C 11. A
12. D 13. C 14. A 15. B 16. D 17. A 18. D 19. C 20. B
21. C 22. D 23. A 24. B 25. C

Spelling Test 6, page 12

1. C 2. C 3. A 4. D 5. B 6. C 7. A 8. B 9. D 10. C 11. A
12. C 13. B 14. D 15. D 16. A 17. B 18. C 19. B 20. D
21. C 22. A 23. A 24. D 25. B

Spelling Test 7, page 13

1. C 2. B 3. D 4. D 5. D 6. B 7. C 8. A 9. C 10. A 11. B
12. D 13. A 14. B 15. D 16. C 17. B 18. A 19. A 20. C
21. D 22. C 23. B 24. A 25. D

Spelling Test 8, page 14

1. C 2. A 3. A 4. D 5. B 6. D 7. A 8. C 9. B 10. D 11. C
12. A 13. B 14. C 15. C 16. A 17. B 18. D 19. B 20. A
21. C 22. D 23. B 24. D 25. A

Spelling Test 9, page 15

1. B 2. C 3. A 4. D 5. C 6. B 7. D 8. A 9. A 10. C 11. B
12. D 13. B 14. A 15. C 16. C 17. D 18. B 19. A 20. C
21. D 22. D 23. A 24. B 25. C

Spelling Test 10, page 16

1. B 2. C 3. A 4. D 5. A 6. B 7. C 8. D 9. B 10. A 11. B
12. C 13. C 14. D 15. A 16. B 17. D 18. C 19. A 20. B
21. C 22. D 23. A 24. D 25. A

Spelling Test 11, page 17

1. D 2. B 3. A 4. C 5. C 6. A 7. B 8. D 9. B 10. C 11. A
12. A 13. D 14. B 15. C 16. B 17. A 18. D 19. C 20. B
21. D 22. A 23. D 24. B 25. C

Spelling Test 12, page 18

1. C 2. D 3. A 4. B 5. B 6. C 7. D 8. A 9. A 10. B 11. D
12. C 13. B 14. B 15. C 16. D 17. A 18. C 19. D 20. B
21. A 22. C 23. D 24. A 25. B

Spelling Test 13, page 19

1. A 2. C 3. B 4. B 5. D 6. C 7. A 8. C 9. A 10. B 11. D
12. D 13. A 14. B 15. C 16. B 17. D 18. C 19. B 20. A
21. D 22. D 23. B 24. A 25. C

Mastering Spelling

Level A • Teacher's Resource Manual

The *Mastering Spelling* program teaches spelling through three proven pedagogical approaches: phonics, structural analysis, and word origins. Every book in the series incorporates short, high-interest spelling lessons; links between spelling and grammar, usage, and mechanics; and real-life applications of spelling skills.

SKILLS OVERVIEW

Spelling patterns and generalizations in the series include:

- Vowel and consonant sounds
- Word endings
- Irregular verbs
- Words with silent letters
- Homophones
- Words from other languages
- Base and root words
- Contractions
- Plural nouns
- Prefixes and suffixes
- Compound words
- Abbreviations
- Related words

For additional vocabulary development and grammar skills, ask your sales representative about these other Globe Fearon programs:

World of Vocabulary

Be A Better Reader

Success in Writing: Grammar Skills for Writers

Globe Fearon Survival Guide for Students

Call 1-800-848-9500 for information.

GLOBE FEARON EDUCATIONAL PUBL

Upper Saddle River, New Jersey

www.globefearon.com